THIS BOOK BELONGS TO:

GUIDEBOOK to the UNKNOWN

A JOURNAL FOR ANXIOUS MINDS

LISA CURRIE

A TARCHERPERIGEE BOOK

tarcherperigee

An imprint of Penguin Random House LLC
penguinrandomhouse.com

TarcherPerigee with tp colophon is a registered trademark of Penguin Random House LLC.

most TarcherPerigee books are available at special quantity discounts for bulk
purchase for sales promotions, premiums, fund-raising, and educational needs.
Special books or book excerpts also can be created to fit specific needs.
For details, write: Specialmarkets@penguinrandomhouse.com.

Library of Congress Control Number: 2022939038

ISBN: 9780593421642

Printed in the United States of America
1st Printing

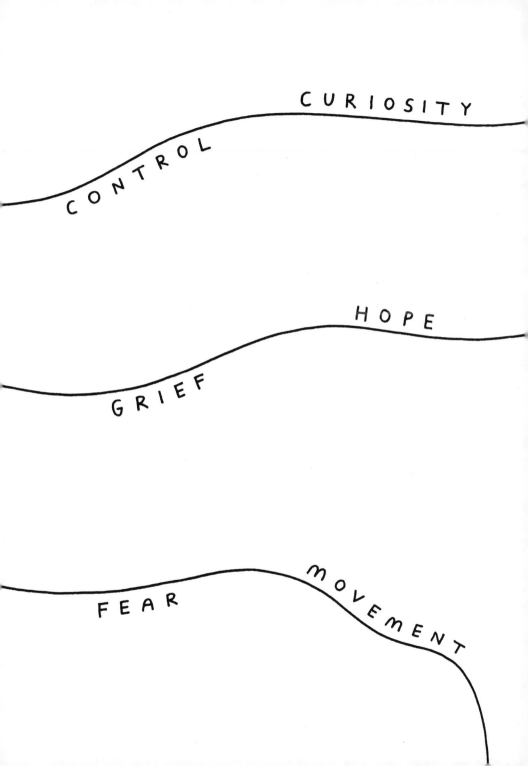

THIS IS A GUIDEBOOK CREATED BY YOU.
PAGE BY PAGE.

THERE ARE SPACES TO GET QUIET WITH
YOURSELF. SPACES TO HONOR WHATEVER
YOU'RE FEELING TODAY. SPACES TO NUDGE
YOUR BODY & MIND IN A NEW DIRECTION.
SPACES TO REMIND YOU OF HOW CAPABLE
YOU ARE & WHAT MAKES A DAY PRECIOUS.

I MADE THIS BOOK FOR YOU & ALSO FOR MY
OWN ANXIOUS MIND. I STILL HAVE BAD DAYS.
DAYS WHEN ANXIETY RUMBLES IN ME & MAKES
MY MIND GO FUZZY. DAYS WHEN I'M SCARED.

I DIDN'T FIND AN ANTIDOTE FOR THESE
UNCOMFORTABLE FEELINGS, BUT I DID
LEARN TO SIT WITH THEM.

I DID LEARN TO UNTANGLE WHAT IS NOT
WITHIN MY CONTROL FROM WHAT IS.

I DID LEARN TO MEET LIFE WHERE IT IS.

I DID LEARN TO SAVOR THE MYSTERY &
CURIOSITY OF BEING ALIVE, RATHER THAN
ALWAYS SCRAMBLING FOR A FEELING OF
CONTROL & CERTAINTY.

I HOPE THIS BOOK MAKES FOR A KIND
COMPANION AS YOU WANDER INTO THE
UNKNOWN TODAY. THANKS FOR BEING HERE!

x lisa

YOU MIGHT LIKE TO WORK THROUGH THIS
BOOK IN ORDER, ONE PAGE AT A TIME.

YOU MIGHT LIKE TO JUST FLICK THROUGH
& SEE WHAT PAGE YOU NEED TODAY.

YOU MIGHT LIKE TO FILL THE PAGES
WITH COLOR & DOODLING!

YOU MIGHT LIKE TO KEEP IT SIMPLER
WITH A PEN & A FEW NOTES JOTTED DOWN.

YOU MIGHT LIKE TO KEEP THIS BOOK
WITHIN REACH FOR WHEN YOU NEED
A FRESH SPLASH OF PERSPECTIVE,
LIKE A FRIEND MIGHT GIVE.

YOU MIGHT LIKE TO CREATE A MORNING
RITUAL FOR YOURSELF, LIKE I DO (SOMETIMES!)
TO CULTIVATE A BIT OF CURIOSITY &
HOPE FOR THE DAY AHEAD.

LOTS OF OPTIONS.
FOR NOW, LET'S TURN THE PAGE & BEGIN!

FIRST, A QUICK CHECK-IN WITH YOURSELF.

<u>ENJOYING</u>:   SAVOR ONE DETAIL THAT'S
RATHER NICE ABOUT THIS
MOMENT (E.G., THE BREEZE
ON MY SHOULDERS AFTER
A HOT DAY).

<u>ENDURING</u>:   WHAT IS ONE THING
WEIGHING ON MY HEART
OR MIND TODAY?

<u>OBSERVING</u>:   ONE DETAIL I CAN SEE,
HEAR OR SMELL AROUND ME,
OR NOTICE ON MY BODY
(E.G., THE TINY HAIRS ON
MY KNUCKLES ARE BLONDE!).

YOU CAN RETURN TO THIS PAGE ANYTIME.

ENJOYING   ENDURING   OBSERVING

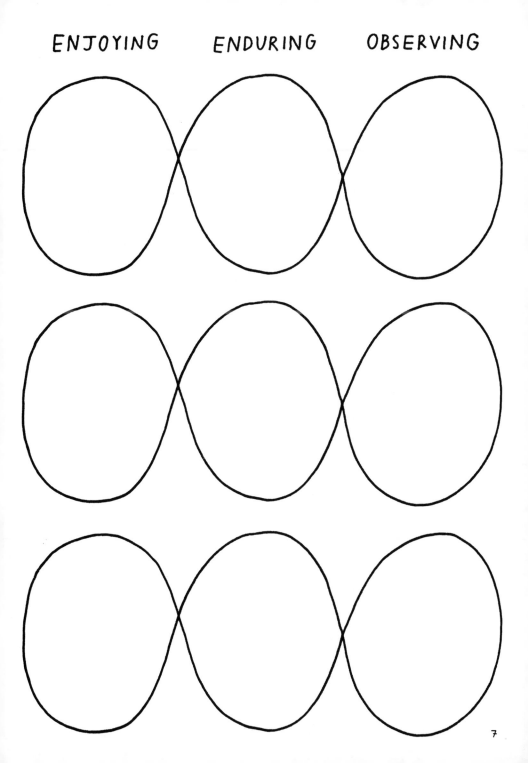

ENJOYING   ENDURING   OBSERVING

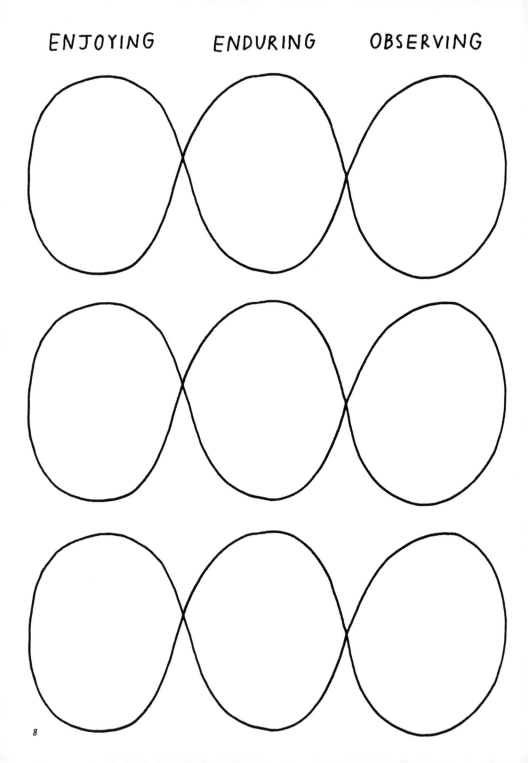

ENJOYING ENDURING OBSERVING

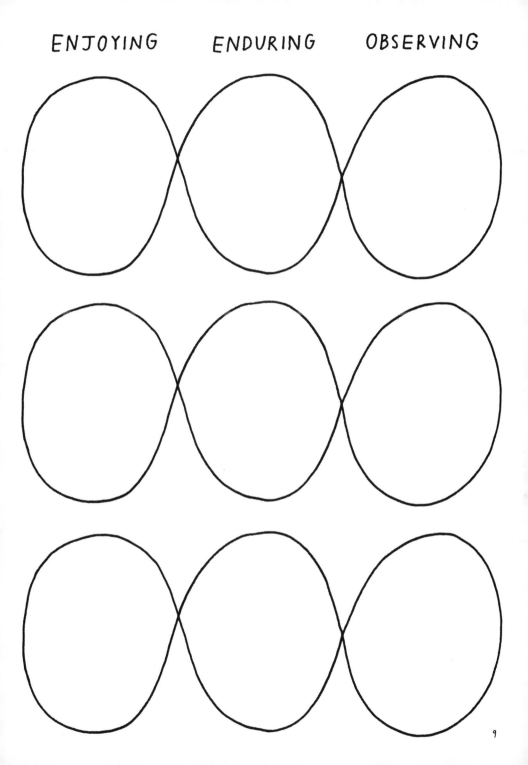

CONTROL

"AS THE STORY GREW,
IT PUT DOWN ROOTS INTO
THE PAST & THREW OUT
UNEXPECTED BRANCHES."

(J.R.R. Tolkien)

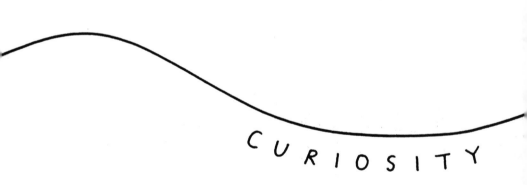

CURIOSITY

WHAT ARE SOME
TIMES THROUGHOUT
MY LIFE WHEN
UNCERTAINTY HAS
BEEN A FRIEND TO ME?

MOMENTS BIG OR TINY, WHEN I WAS
DELIGHTED BY THE MYSTERIES OF LIFE
OR JUST PLEASANTLY SURPRISED AT
THE WAY THINGS UNFOLDED?

IN WHAT WAYS
HAS THE UNKNOWN
BEEN A FRIEND
TO ME LATELY?

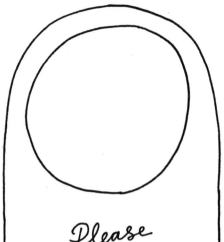

Please
~~DO NOT~~
DISTURB

A WELCOME
INTERRUPTION

A RECENT
TICKLE OF
CURIOSITY

AN UNEXPECTED GIFT

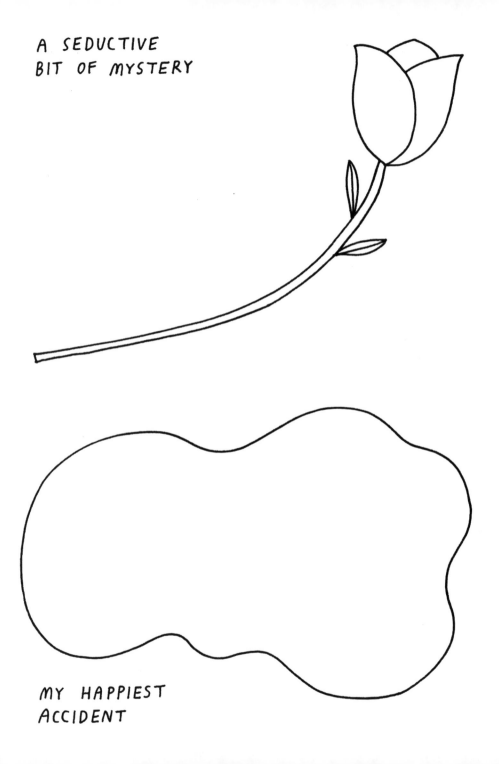

A SEDUCTIVE
BIT OF MYSTERY

MY HAPPIEST
ACCIDENT

A THRILLING DISCOVERY

GOOD NEWS WE DIDN'T SEE COMING

WHEN I'M RIDING A WAVE OF ANXIETY,
WHERE DOES IT USUALLY TAKE ME TO?
WHAT ARE THE THINGS I END UP DOING?

WHAT ARE SOME GOOD WAYS I'VE FOUND
TO DROP ANCHOR WHEN I NEED TO?
WHAT ARE SOME THINGS THAT STEADY
ME & BRING ME BACK TO MYSELF?

WHAT'S ONE THING I NEVER REGRET
SHOWING UP FOR, EVEN IF IT'S HARD
TO GET MYSELF THERE OR BEGIN?

WHAT DOES THE AFTERGLOW FEEL
LIKE EXACTLY? IN WHAT WAYS DO
I NOTICE MY BODY & MIND HAVE
SHIFTED A BIT?

MY ANXIETY IS SHOUTING THESE
THOUGHTS & WORRIES AT ME TODAY

IF I PAUSE
FOR A MOMENT

& TAKE A FEW
DEEP BREATHS,

MY INSTINCT
WHISPERS...

IF I WERE TO STITCH
A LITTLE SQUARE OF
MY DAY TODAY, WHAT
MIGHT THAT LOOK LIKE?

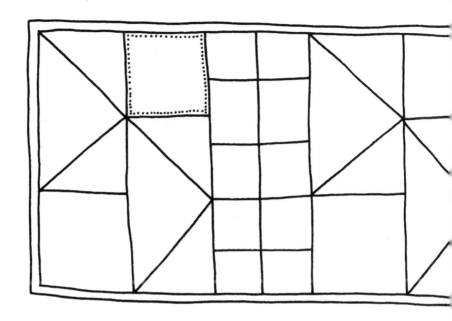

WHAT IF I <u>ZOOM OUT</u>?

WHAT DOES THE REST OF MY
QUILT LOOK LIKE?

THE QUILT OF MY WEEK.
THE QUILT OF MY MONTH.
THE QUILT OF THIS SEASON.
THE QUILT OF MY ENTIRE LIFETIME...

HOW MIGHT THIS ONE LITTLE SQUARE
FIT AMONG THE WHOLE EXPANSIVE,
ECLECTIC QUILT?

SOME OF THE <u>BEST</u> CARDS I'VE
BEEN DEALT IN MY LIFE SO FAR

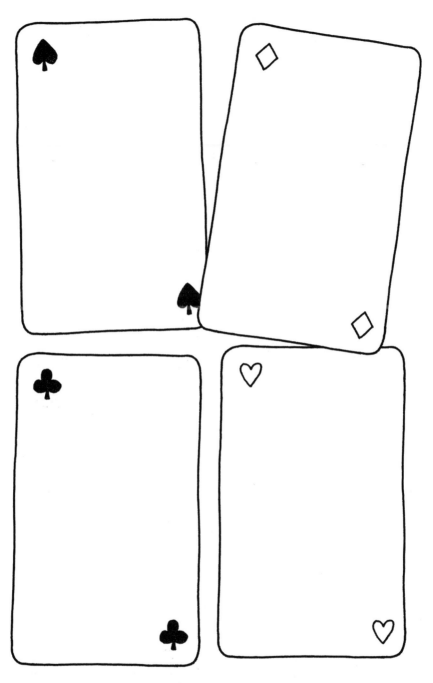

A FEW OF THE CARDS I _WORRY_ ABOUT
BEING DEALT IN THE FUTURE

THE CARDS I'M THANKFUL TO
BE HOLDING TODAY

THE CARDS I <u>HOPE</u> TO HOLD SOMEDAY
(EVEN IF ONLY MOMENTARILY)

THE ONE CARD I ALWAYS
HAVE UP MY SLEEVE

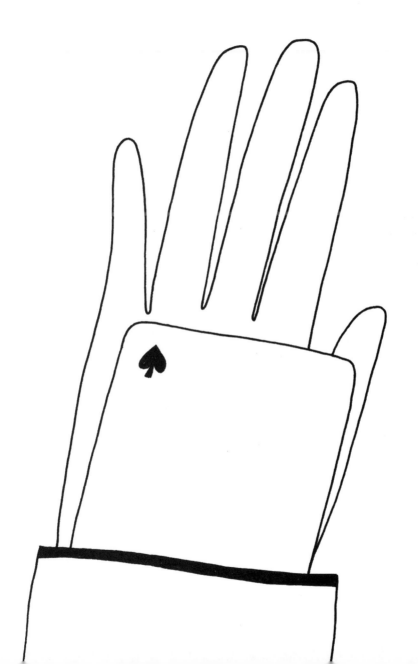

IF I KNEW THEY'D SAY YES,
WHAT WOULD I ASK FOR TODAY?

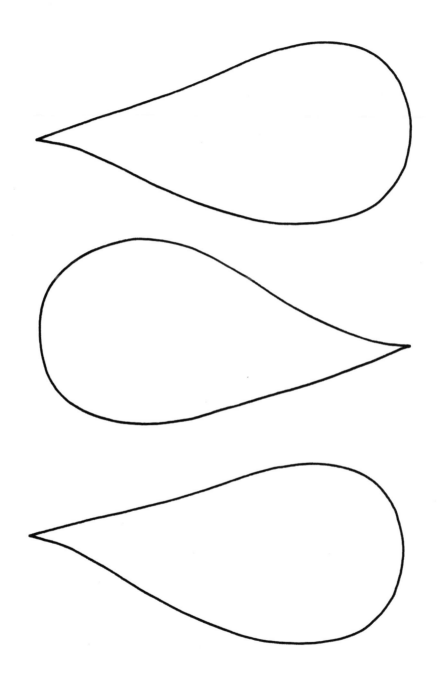

IF I REFLECT ON MOMENTS IN MY LIFE
WHEN I HAD REAL FUN & FELT SO ALIVE,
WHAT ARE A FEW THAT COME TO MIND?

IF I REFLECT ON <u>HOW</u> I MADE MY WAY INTO
THOSE MOMENTS, WHAT BOLD MOVES DID
I MAKE? WHAT CURIOSITIES DID I FOLLOW?
DID ANYTHING HAVE TO GO "WRONG" FIRST?

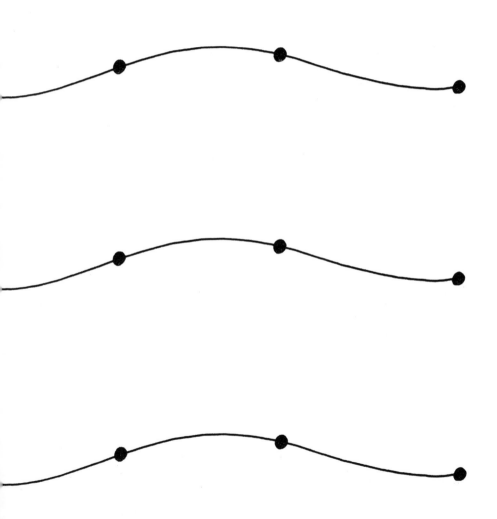

WHERE MIGHT MY CURIOSITY
LEAD ME IF I FOLLOWED
IT WHOLEHEARTEDLY?

WHAT ARE SOME UNMARKED DOORS
I'VE BEEN CURIOUS TO OPEN?

HAVE-DONES

COULD-DOS

EXPERIMENTS IN VICARIOUS JOY

WHAT MIGHT BE SOME OF
THE QUIET, UNTOLD SWEETNESS
GOING ON AROUND ME RIGHT NOW?

PERHAPS A NEIGHBOR STANDS
BAREFOOT IN THEIR KITCHEN
& BITES INTO A PEACH THAT
IS PERFECTLY RIPE!

SOMEONE JUST SOLVED THEIR
FIRST CROSSWORD PUZZLE
& IS CELEBRATING WITH
A LITTLE DANCE IN THEIR CHAIR!

COULD I TRAIN MY IMAGINATION
TO THINK OF NOT ONLY THE
WORST (AS IT IS SO GOOD AT DOING)
BUT ALSO THE BEST OF US?

SWEETNESSES NOT POSTED ONLINE,
BUT SAVORED QUIETLY
& TUCKED AWAY AS THE TINY
MIRACLE OF THEIR DAY.

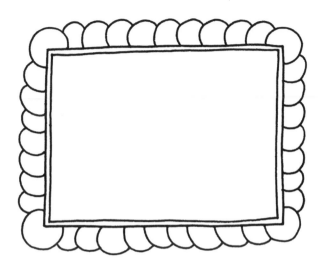

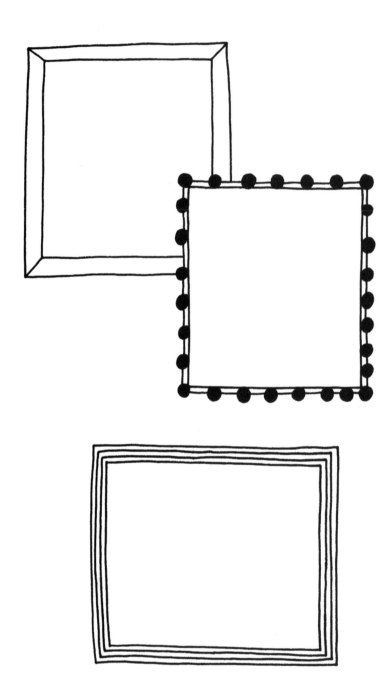

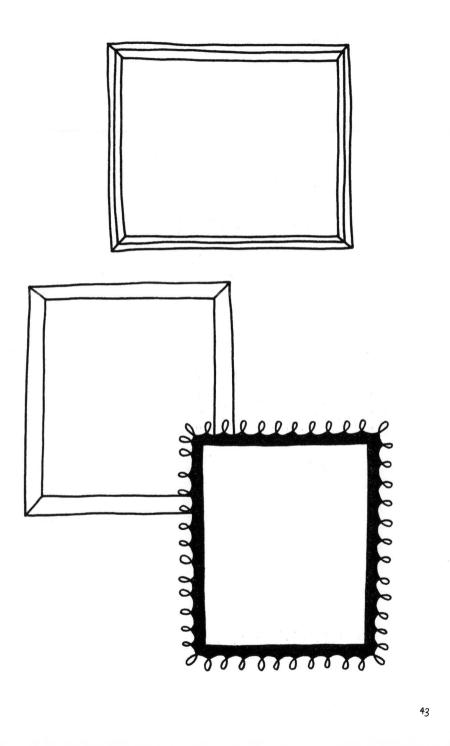

STORAGE FOR THE CONCERNS & UNCERTAINTIES THAT ARE BEYOND MY CONTROL TODAY

45

GENERATE

THINGS I DO THAT LEAVE ME
ON A HIGH—THAT ACTUALLY
ENERGIZE ME

CONSERVE

THINGS I DO THAT RELAX
& NOURISH ME

DRAIN

THINGS I DO THAT CAN BE
NUMBING & LEAVE ME FEELING
SORT OF EMPTY AFTER

THE ITCH

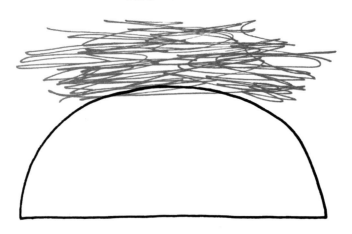

THE ACHE

IT'S FINE TO SCRATCH AN ITCH!
TO DO THE THING THAT FEELS GOOD
& GIVES US AN INSTANT SENSE
OF RELIEF & COMFORT.

BUT SITTING BELOW THE ITCH IS
SOMETIMES AN ACHE WE'RE NOT
TENDING TO. AN UNCOMFORTABLE
FEELING WE'RE TRYING TO AVOID
OR A TENDER NEED WE'RE
SCARED TO VOICE.

WE CAN SCRATCH THE ITCH,
BUT THE ACHE IS STILL THERE.

IF WE TRY TO NAME THE ACHE,
IT MEANS WE CAN SIT WITH IT
FOR A MOMENT, HAND ON OUR
CHEST, DEEP BREATH, AND SAY
"I SEE YOU & IT'S OK YOU'RE HERE".

MAYBE THAT'S ENOUGH FOR NOW.

WHAT'S THE ITCH?
AND MORE IMPORTANTLY,
WHAT'S THE ACHE?

THE ITCH

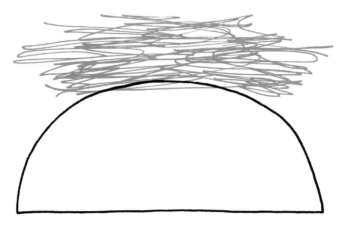

THE ACHE

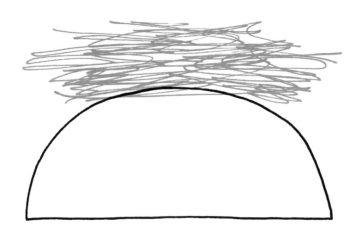

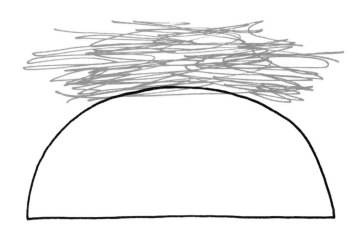

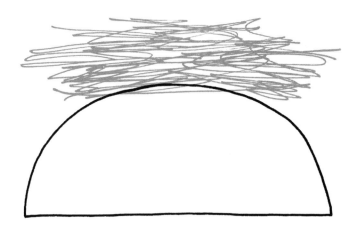

GRIEF

"TO BE LOVING IS TO
BE OPEN TO GRIEF,
TO BE TOUCHED BY
SORROW, EVEN SORROW
THAT IS UNENDING."

(bell hooks)

" HOPE RISES OUT OF
KNOWN SUFFERING &
IS THE DEFIANT &
DISSENTING SPARK
THAT REFUSES TO
BE EXTINGUISHED. "

(Nick Cave)

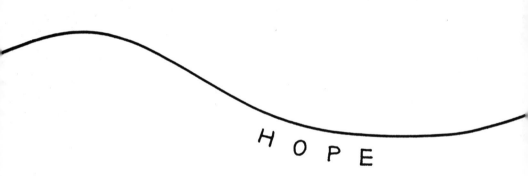

H   O   P   E

WHAT IS WEIGHING
ON MY HEART TODAY?

"LIGHT" A CANDLE & SIT IN
THE UNCOMFORTABLE FOR A MOMENT.

SIT WITH YOUR EMPATHY, YOUR GRIEF,
YOUR TENDER & COMPLICATED HUMAN HEART.

FEEL WHATEVER IT IS YOU NEED TO
LET YOURSELF FEEL RIGHT NOW.

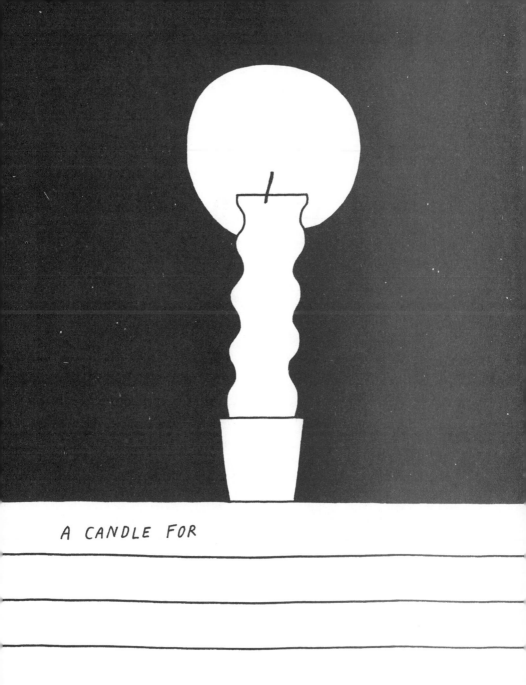

A CANDLE FOR

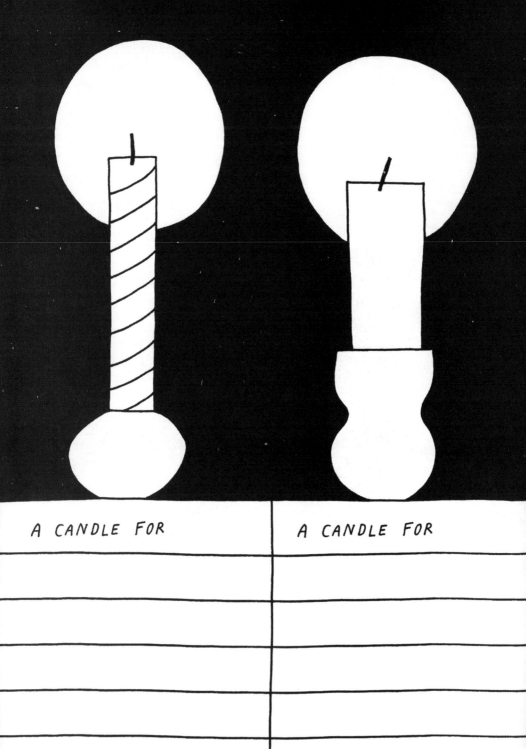

A CANDLE FOR

A CANDLE FOR

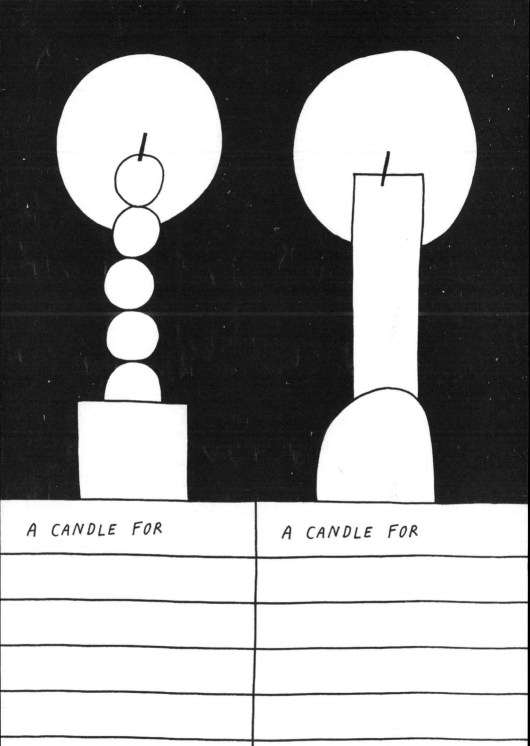

A CANDLE FOR

A CANDLE FOR

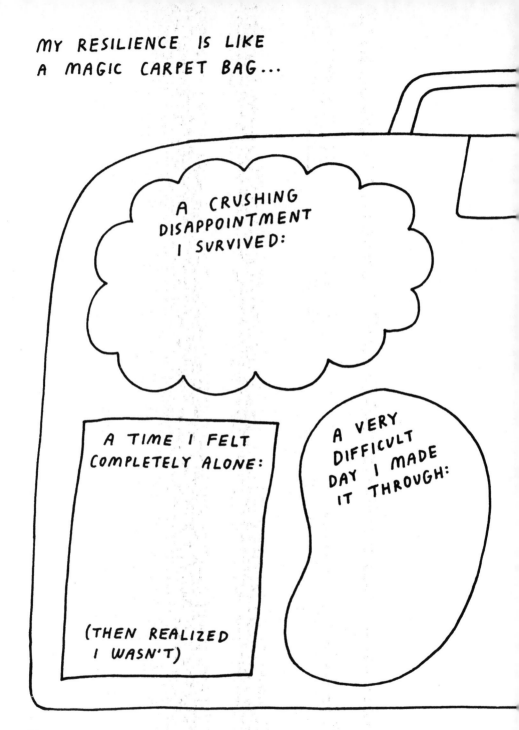

FOUR THINGS I "SHOULD" DO THAT I GIVE MYSELF PERMISSION TO FAIL AT THIS WEEK

THREE QUALITIES I ADMIRE IN OTHERS & ALSO SEE IN MYSELF

WHAT INSPIRES FEELINGS OF
AWE & WONDER IN ME?

THE GLOW OF A FULL MOON?
A PIECE OF MUSIC THAT MOVES ME?

WHEN MY INNER DIALOGUE BEGINS
TO SPIRAL, WHAT ARE THE SIGHTS
& SOUNDS I CAN TRUST TO TAKE ME
BEYOND MYSELF FOR A MOMENT?

ONCE UPON A TIME

A LINEAR FUTURE

ARE THERE ANY PRESSURES I FEEL TO
REACH CERTAIN MILESTONES AT A CERTAIN
AGE OR IN A CERTAIN ORDER?

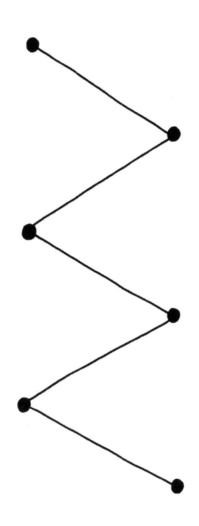

A NEBULOUS FUTURE

WHAT IF INSTEAD I IMAGINED MY FUTURE
AS AN EVER—SHIFTING GALAXY OF POSSIBILITIES
TO EXPLORE? WHAT MIGHT THAT LOOK LIKE?

A LIST OF THINGS TO LOOK FORWARD TO

IN A FEW HOURS

$\longrightarrow$

A COUPLE OF DAYS
FROM NOW

$\longrightarrow$

NEXT MONTH

$\longrightarrow$

NEXT SEASON

$\longrightarrow$

SOMEDAY!

$\longrightarrow$

THE SANDCASTLES OF MY DAY

HONORING (& SEEKING OUT) EPHEMERAL
PLEASURES! WHAT SMALL GESTURES
LATELY HAVE INSPIRED A FLEETING
MOMENT OF CONNECTION OR DELIGHT?

WHAT ARE SOME OF THE SENSORY DELIGHTS I SAVORED AS A CHILD?

SIGHT

SOUND

TASTE

TOUCH

WHAT ARE SOME OF THE SENSORY DELIGHTS I COULD BE SAVORING NOW?

WE CAN BE IN SUCH A HURRY TO
ATTACH MEANING TO A MOMENT
   (WE'RE SO LUCKY! THIS IS FUN!
ISN'T THIS FUN! IT'S SO BEAUTIFUL!)
BECAUSE, I THINK, ON SOME LEVEL
IT FEELS LIKE CONTROL. I ALREADY
HAVE THIS MOMENT ALL FIGURED
OUT, NOTHING CAN SURPRISE ME!

BUT WE SHINE A LIGHT SO BRIGHT
ON THE SCENE THAT IT LOSES ALL
ITS BEAUTIFUL DETAIL. WE SLAP ON
MEANING BEFORE THE MOMENT HAS
EVEN HAD A CHANCE TO BLOOM.

SO I REMIND MY ANXIOUS MIND
TO JUST OBSERVE WHAT IS HERE
          IN FRONT OF ME.

          WHAT AM I SEEING?
WHAT AM I FEELING IN MY BODY?
   THE COLORS, THE TEXTURES,
   THE SENSATIONS, THE DETAILS.

     FORGET ABOUT THE MEANING
FOR NOW, JUST OBSERVE WHAT IS.

DAILY OBSERVATIONS

THE COLOR PALETTE
OF A STRANGER'S OUTFIT

A VERY FAMILIAR
THING I SAW IN
A NEW WAY

AN INTERESTING
TEXTURE

THREE SOUNDS I TUNED IN TO

"IT'S LIKE DRIVING A CAR
AT NIGHT: YOU NEVER SEE
FURTHER THAN YOUR HEADLIGHTS,
BUT YOU CAN MAKE THE
WHOLE TRIP THAT WAY."

(E. L. Doctorow)

IF MY MIND IS SCRAMBLING TO FIGURE
IT ALL OUT & SEE BEYOND THE HEADLIGHTS,
CAN I GENTLY BRING IT BACK TO WHAT'S
RIGHT IN FRONT OF ME? WHAT WILL
I GIVE MY ATTENTION TO TODAY?

WHAT ARE THE RITUALS IN MY DAY
(OR WEEK) THAT OFFER A FEELING
OF CONTROL AMID THE UNCERTAINTY?

WHAT ARE THE RITUALS IN MY
DAY (OR WEEK) THAT INVITE A BIT
OF PLAY & SURPRISE?

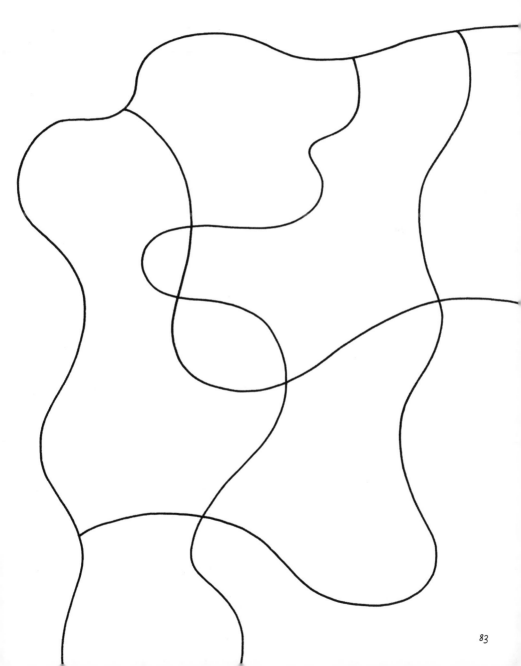

IN TIMES OF UNCERTAINTY,
WHO DO I HAVE ALONGSIDE ME?

Dear _____

I feel so lucky to have you with me as we discover the lives that are coming to us. You bring the _____, I'll bring the _____

X X

Dear _____

Will you join me on this voyage into the unknown? Together we can _____ _____ and maybe even _____

X X

WAYS I SHOW UP & CARE FOR
THE PEOPLE I LOVE

WAYS I SHOW UP & CARE FOR MYSELF

WHAT ARE THE STORIES
I TELL MYSELF ABOUT WHO I AM?

①

A STORY THAT TENDS TO GET IN MY WAY,
THAT I MAYBE DON'T SAY ALOUD, THAT
MAKES ME FEEL ROTTEN AT THE CORE.

②

A STORY THAT BOLSTERS ME WHEN I STEP
OUT INTO THE WORLD & FEELS LIKE THE
BEST VERSION OF MYSELF.

③

A STORY I WAS HANDED BY SOMEONE ELSE
& SEEM TO HAVE HELD ON TO.

④

A STORY I'D LIKE TO TRY ON,
TO SEE HOW IT FEELS!

TEN YEARS FROM NOW, LOOKING BACK,
WHAT MIGHT I WISH I'D DONE <u>MORE OF</u>
IN THIS SEASON OF MY LIFE?

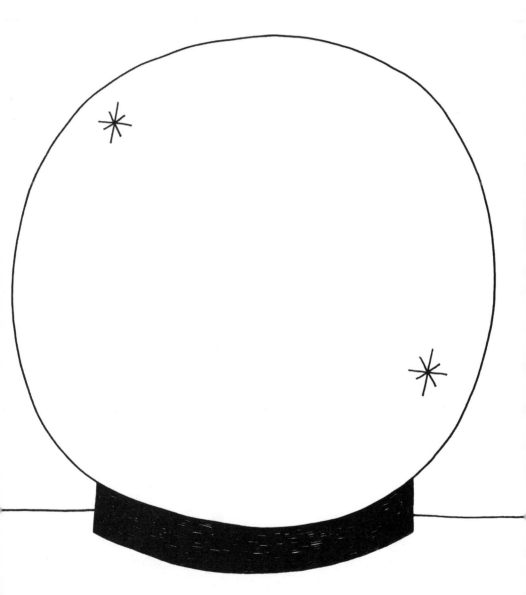

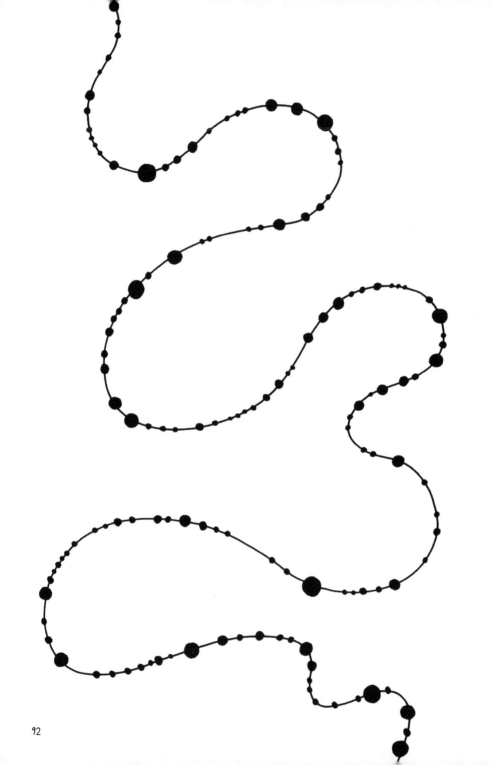

I IMAGINE MY LIFE AS AN
ENDLESS STRING OF KNOTS
TO UNTANGLE — SOME LOOSER
& UNRAVELED WITH EASE,
OTHERS CHUNKIER & IN NEED
OF REAL GRIT.

WHEN I SEE MY LIFE THIS WAY,
I NOTICE THE EMPTY SPACES
BETWEEN THE KNOTS & WONDER
HOW I MIGHT ENJOY
THAT SPACE TOO.

IF THE STRING OF LIFE
IS ENDLESSLY KNOTTY,
WHAT'S MY RUSH IN GETTING
TO THE NEXT ONE?

WHETHER IT'S FOR TEN MINUTES
OR A WHOLE WEEKEND, HOW MANY
WAYS CAN I THINK OF TO RELISH
THOSE SPACES BETWEEN THE KNOTS?

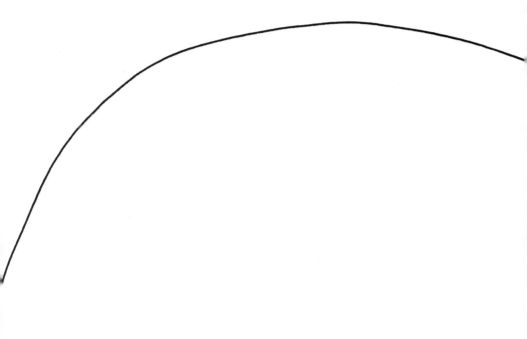

WHAT ARE SOME THOUGHTS OR WORRIES
YOU'VE BEEN FIXATING ON LATELY?

IMAGINE THE WORRY IS A BUBBLE
RESTING ON YOUR HAND.

BREATHE IN DEEPLY & GENTLY BLOW
THE BUBBLE AWAY.

WATCH IT PEACEFULLY DRIFT UP
TOWARD THE ROOF OR SKY
& EVENTUALLY GIVE A SATISFYING POP

(LITTLE VISUALIZATIONS LIKE THIS CAN HELP TO
INTERRUPT THE RUMINATION & LET OUR MINDS
KNOW IT'S OK, WE'VE DONE ALL WE CAN FOR NOW)

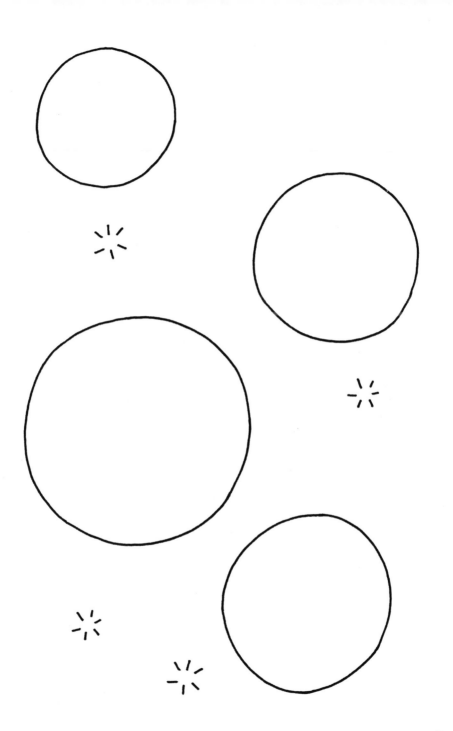

WHAT DO I FEEL ARE THE "MISSING PIECES"
IN MY LIFE RIGHT NOW? IF I COULD JUST
____ & ____ THEN LIFE WOULD BE COMPLETE!

WHAT IF THIS LIFE I HAVE RIGHT NOW
IS COMPLETE? WHAT MAKES IT SO?
WHAT MAKES IT ENOUGH?

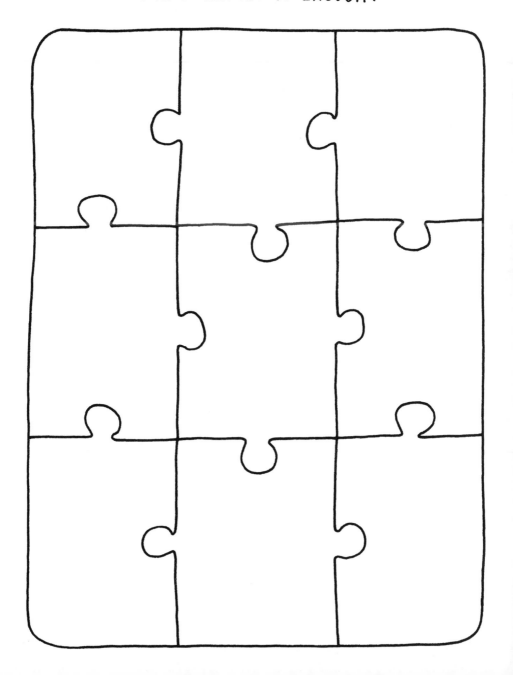

NOSTALGIC SMELLS

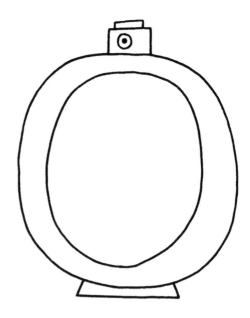

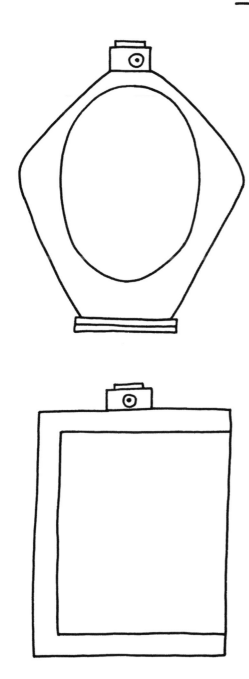

RATHER THAN ALWAYS TRYING
TO FIGURE OUT WHAT I WANT
FROM LIFE, WHY NOT ASK
THE SIMPLER, GENTLER QUESTION—
WHAT MIGHT LIFE WANT FROM ME?

WHAT ARE THE OPPORTUNITIES
FOR COMMUNITY & CONNECTION
I KEEP WALKING BY?

TUNING IN TO THE RHYTHMS OF NATURE

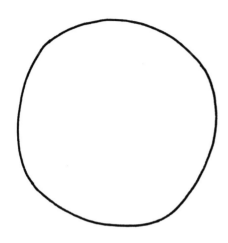

HOW FULL IS
THE MOON
TONIGHT?

(GO OUTSIDE TO
SEE FOR YOURSELF.)

FROM WHERE I AM NOW, WHICH DIRECTION
DOES THE SUN RISE IN THE MORNING?
& SET IN THE EVENING?

WHERE ARE SOME GOOD SPOTS
TO WATCH IT FROM?

WHAT FRUITS & VEGETABLES ARE IN SEASON AT THE MOMENT?

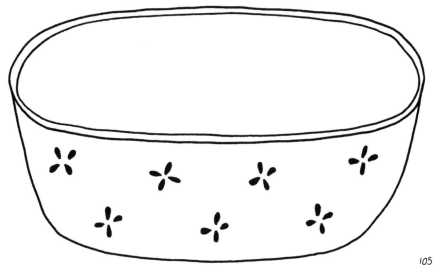

I SEE YOU
TRYING

WHAT MOMENTS OF TRYING
WOULD I LOVE TO
BE SEEN IN TODAY?

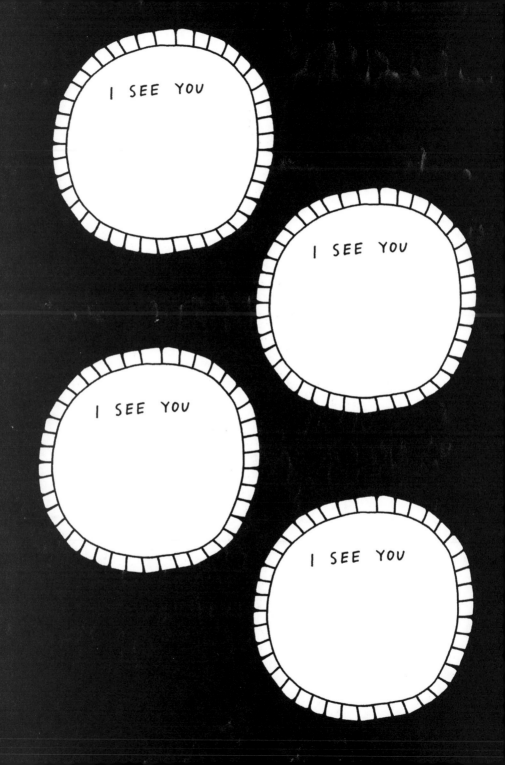

FEAR

"THE WHOLE FUTURE
LIES IN UNCERTAINTY:
LIVE IMMEDIATELY."

(Seneca)

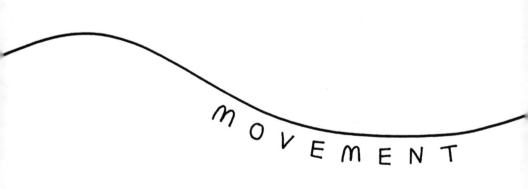

MOVEMENT

IN WHAT WAYS DOES MY PHYSICAL SELF
RESPOND TO ANXIETY? DO I CURL INWARD?
STAY SMALL? RETREAT AWAY FROM THE WORLD?

WHAT IF RATHER THAN TRY TO "TALK" MYSELF OUT OF ANXIETY, I LED WITH MY BODY? WHAT MIGHT THAT LOOK LIKE, TO PHYSICALLY EXPAND & GROW?

I COULD START SMALL. GENTLY OUTSTRETCH MY ARMS TO FEEL THE BREEZE. LIFT MY EYES TO SEE HOW EXPANSIVE THE SKY IS. PUT ON A WILD TUNE & THROW MY LIMBS AROUND WITH ABANDON!

WHEN I'M ANXIOUS IT FEELS SAFER TO
GET SMALLER. BUT REALLY, WHEN I'M NOT
IN IMMEDIATE DANGER, ISN'T IT SAFER
TO EXPAND? GROW MY COMMUNITY.
MAKE MORE MEANINGFUL CONNECTIONS
WITH PEOPLE. KEEP MY EYES UP & AWARE
OF WHAT'S AROUND ME.

WHAT ARE SOME MOVEMENTS I CAN
MAKE OUTWARD TO EXPAND & GROW?
(RATHER THAN SHRINK & FADE)

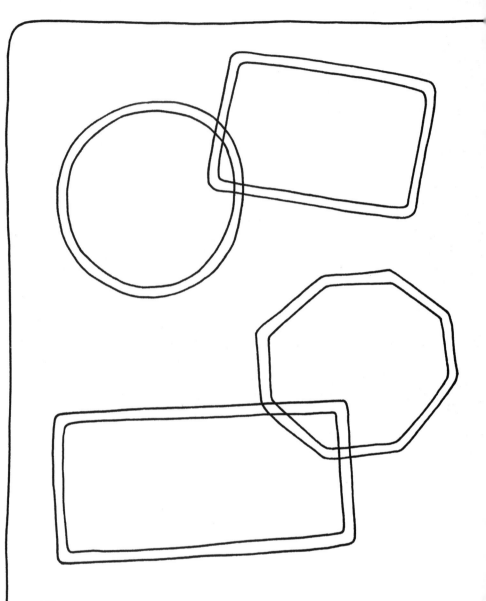

IF I WERE MOVING TOWARD PLEASURE
& FUN, WHAT WOULD I INCORPORATE
MORE OF INTO MY DAYS?

PLEASURE
PASSPORT

WHEN WE DAYDREAM ABOUT OUR
FUTURE SELVES WE TEND TO IMAGINE
HOW WE WANT OUR LIVES TO LOOK.

INSTEAD... WHATEVER SHAPE MY LIFE
ENDS UP TAKING, HOW DO I HOPE TO FEEL?

THEN IN WHAT SMALL WAYS
COULD I FEEL THAT WAY TODAY?
IN WHAT SMALL WAYS ARE THOSE
FEELINGS ALREADY AVAILABLE TO ME?

HOPES FOR MY FUTURE

HELD LIGHTLY,
WITH A GENTLE CURIOSITY.

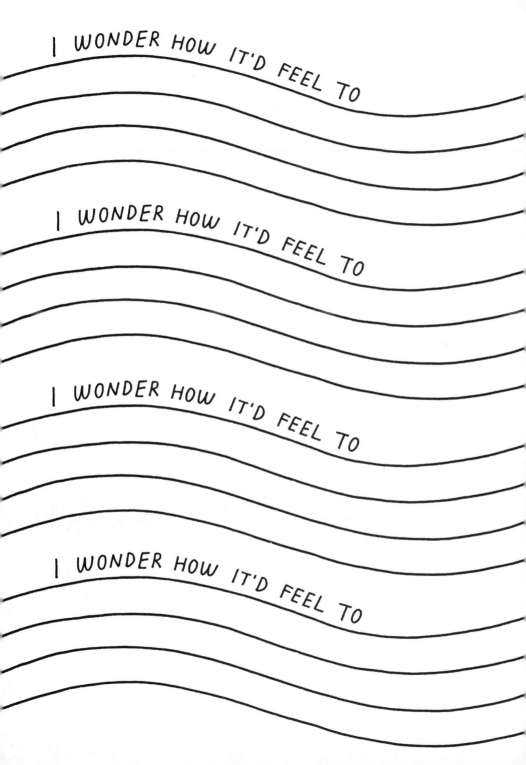

THERE IS NO
SHAME IN FAILURE
OR MISTAKES.

I CAN MAKE A WRONG
DECISION (OR HAVE
THINGS NOT WORK OUT
HOW I HOPED) & STILL

TRUST MYSELF.

A NOTE TO SELF

WHO AM I IN THIS MOMENT?

MY EVER-SHIFTING SELF.

ALWAYS A WORK IN PROGRESS.
ALWAYS ENOUGH.

WHAT ARE MY FIRST IMPRESSIONS
OF THE SELF I AM MEETING HERE NOW?

SO FAMILIAR TO ME,
BUT STILL ABLE TO SURPRISE.

WHAT DO I SEE IN THEM THAT MAYBE
I HAVEN'T QUITE NOTICED BEFORE?

WHO AM I? (IN THIS MOMENT)

WHO WAS I? (IN A MOMENT PAST)

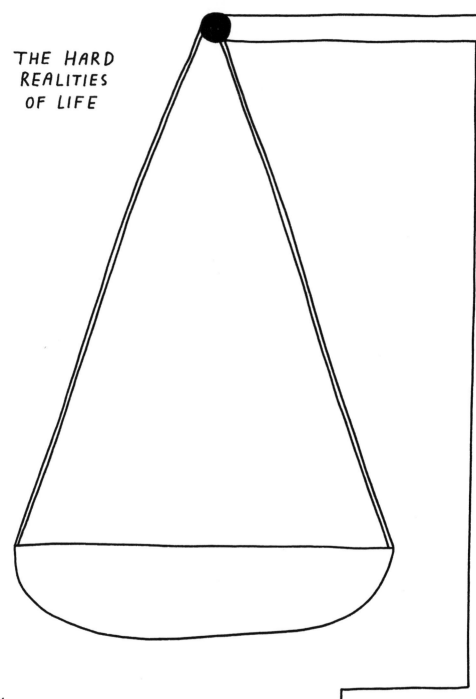

THE HARD
REALITIES
OF LIFE

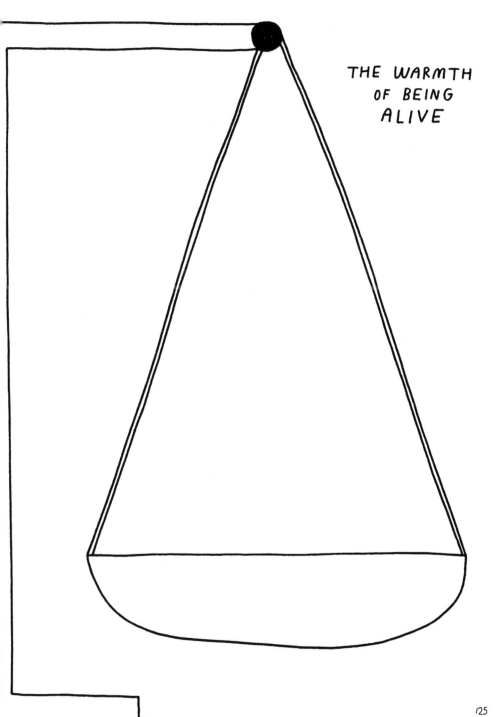

THE WARMTH
OF BEING
ALIVE

THE SILENT CONVERSATIONS I'VE
BEEN HAVING WITH MYSELF LATELY,
ARE THEY USUALLY PEP TALKS
OR PUT-DOWNS?

AM I ADVENTURING INTO THE
UNKNOWN WITH A COMPASSIONATE,
SUPPORTIVE TEAMMATE?
OR A BULLY WHO KEEPS KICKING
ME WHEN I'm DOWN?

IT CAN BE A LIFELONG PRACTICE
TO IMBUE OUR INNER VOICE
WITH SELF-COMPASSION,
TO TALK TO OURSELVES AS
WE WOULD TO A FRIEND.

KIND WORDS I CAN OFFER
MYSELF TODAY ⟶

STORAGE FOR THE CONCERNS & UNCERTAINTIES THAT ARE BEYOND MY CONTROL TODAY

129

MY ANXIETY IS SHOUTING THESE
THOUGHTS & WORRIES AT ME TODAY

IF I PAUSE
FOR A MOMENT

& TAKE A FEW
DEEP BREATHS,

MY INSTINCT
WHISPERS...

I'M CHOOSING TO SAY "YES"
BECAUSE...

"BE PATIENT TOWARDS ALL THAT IS
UNSOLVED IN YOUR HEART & TRY
TO LOVE THE QUESTIONS THEMSELVES,
LIKE LOCKED ROOMS & LIKE BOOKS THAT
ARE WRITTEN IN A VERY FOREIGN TONGUE...

THE POINT IS, TO LIVE EVERYTHING.
LIVE THE QUESTIONS NOW.

PERHAPS YOU WILL THEN GRADUALLY,
WITHOUT NOTICING IT, LIVE ALONG SOME
DISTANT DAY INTO THE ANSWER."

(Rainer Maria Rilke)

OF ALL THAT IS UNSOLVED
IN MY HEART, WHAT QUESTION
DO I WANT TO MOVE TOWARD?

WHAT QUESTION DO I WANT TO
START LIVING TODAY?

A TREE SWAYS & SHAKES IN THE WIND.
BELOW THE GROUND, OUT OF SIGHT, ITS ROOTS
TRAVEL DEEP & STRONG INTO THE EARTH.

WHAT DO I FEEL ARE MY ROOTS?
WHAT KEEPS ME STRONG & STEADY
FROM THE INSIDE?

HOW MIGHT I TEND TO MY ROOTS ON
CALMER DAYS, TO PREPARE FOR WHEN
THE STORMS ROLL BY?

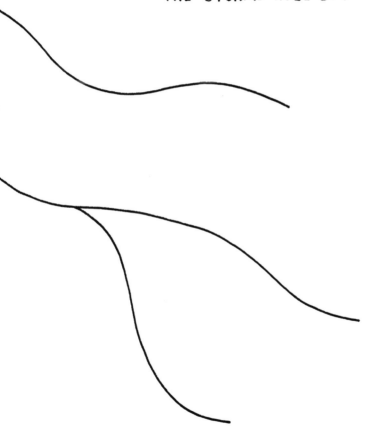

BREATHE IN SLOWLY
LIKE YOU'RE SMELLING
A LOVELY FLOWER...

HOLD FOR THREE SECONDS...

THEN BREATHE OUT
GENTLY LIKE YOU'RE
BLOWING OUT A CANDLE.

(REPEAT x 3)

THESE ARE LITTLE INVITATIONS TO PAUSE
FOR A FEW SECONDS & CONNECT WITH
YOUR BREATH. CUT THEM OUT & STICK ONTO
YOUR BATHROOM MIRROR, BESIDE THE KETTLE,
ANYWHERE YOU COULD USE THE REMINDER!

LIKE A BLURRY POLAROID PHOTO SLOWLY
DEVELOPING, WHAT IN MY LIFE RIGHT NOW
NEEDS ONLY PATIENCE?

PERHAPS LIFE IS SORT OF LIKE
A POTLUCK. I CAN'T CONTROL WHAT
OTHER PEOPLE (OR LIFE IN GENERAL)
BRING TO THE TABLE. IT'S A FEAST
OF DISAPPOINTMENT & DELIGHT!

THE ONLY THING I <u>CAN</u> CONTROL IS WHETHER
I SHOW UP TO THE PARTY OR NOT,
& WHAT WILL I BRING TO SHARE?

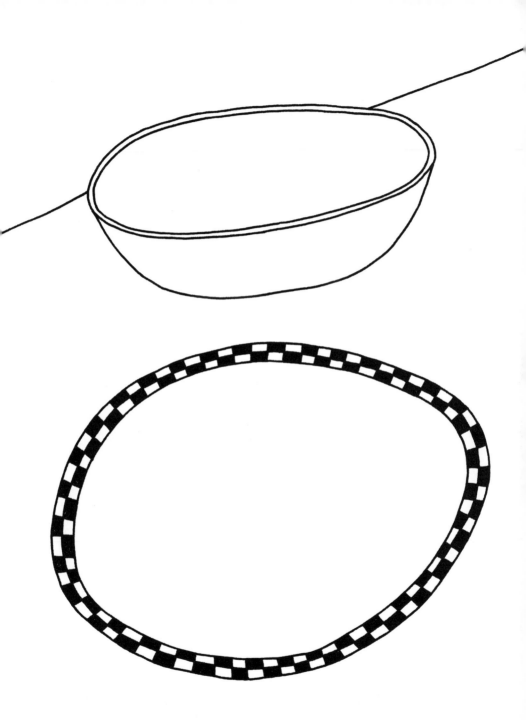

NOTES & OBSERVATIONS

NOTES & OBSERVATIONS

NOTES & OBSERVATIONS

NOTES & OBSERVATIONS

LISA CURRIE IS A BIG BELIEVER
IN THE CATHARTIC MAGIC OF
PUTTING PEN TO PAPER.
SHE SAYS HI TO THE MOON FROM
MELBOURNE (NAARM), AUSTRALIA.

FOR MORE!
LISACURRIE.COM

THANKS MUM FOR INSPIRING ME WITH
YOUR LOVE OF VISUAL METAPHOR.

THANKS DAVID & ROBIN FOR THE SPACE
AT MANALLACK STUDIOS.

THANKS SORCHE, MARIAN & THE TEAM
AT TARCHERPERIGEE!